Animal Baby Sitters

Animal Baby Sitters

Gail Jarrow and Dr. Paul Sherman

LIBRARY

Franklin Watts
A Division of Scholastic Inc.
New York • Toronto • London • Auckland • Sydney
Mexico City • New Delhi • Hong Kong
Danbury, Connecticut

For my offspring: Kyle, Tate, and Heather — G.J.
For my baby sitters: Barb, Ron, Uncle Barry, and Uncle Marty — P.S.

Note to readers: Definitions for words in **bold** can be found in the Glossary at the back of this book.

Photographs ©: Animals Animals: 42 (Dani/Jeske), 5 left, 30, 36, 37 (Hamman/Heldring), 51 (J & B Photographers), 5 right, 12, 18 (Johnny Johnson), 44, 46 (Raymond A. Mendez), 35 (Stefan Meyers), 16 (Leonard Lee Rue III); BBC Natural History Unit/Jeff Foott: 2; Dembinsky Photo Assoc.: 40, 41 (Wendy Dennis), 8 (Anthony Mercieca), 26 (Stan Osolinski), cover (Anup Shah); Frank Staub: 6; Minden Pictures/Mitsuaki Iwago: 15; Peter Arnold Inc./Dianne Blell: 10; Photo Researchers, NY: 45 (Toni Angermayer DGPH), 9 (Scott Camazine), 53 (Tim Davis), 38 (Clem Haagner), 19, 20, 50 (Tom McHugh), 32 (Richard Parker), 28 (Gregory K. Scott), 24 (H.A. Thorhill); Visuals Unlimited: 48 (Elizabeth DeLaney), 34 (Ken Lucas), 17, 22 (Joe McDonald), 14 (Fritz Pölking).

The photograph on the cover shows a lioness carrying a cub. The photograph opposite the title page shows an adult prairie dog with a young prairie dog.

Library of Congress Cataloging-in-Publication Data

Jarrow, Gail
    Animal baby sitters / by Gail Jarrow and Paul Sherman.
       p.   cm.— (Watts Library)
    Includes bibliographical references and index.
    ISBN 0-531-11881-9 (lib. bdg.)   0-531-16571-X (pbk.)
    1. Cooperative breeding in animals—Juvenile literature. 2. Parental Behavior in animals. 3. Animals—Habits and behavior. I. Sherman, Paul W. 1949– II. Title. III. Series.
QL751.5 .J37 2001
591.56'3 —dc21   00-039929
                                                                                                                  CIP

© 2001 Franklin Watts, a division of Scholastic Inc.
All rights reserved. Published simultaneously in Canada.
Printed in the United States of America.
1 2 3 4 5 6 7 8 9 10 R 10 09 08 07 06 05 04 03 02 01

Contents

Chapter One
Helpers on Duty 7

Chapter Two
Moms Helping Moms 13

Chapter Three
Family Ties in the Air 23

Chapter Four
Staying Home with Mom and Dad 31

Chapter Five
Safety in Numbers 39

Chapter Six
Why Do They Help? 49

54 **Glossary**

56 **To Find Out More**

59 **A Note on Sources**

61 **Index**

Most spiders lay many eggs, then leave the young spiders to develop on their own. Many animal parents don't take care of their young at all.

Chapter One

Helpers on Duty

Most animal parents never need a baby sitter. In fact, they don't stay with their offspring long enough to raise them. Their parenting stops after they contribute the eggs or sperm that develop into young animals.

Fish, amphibians, reptiles, and insects all produce large numbers of young. Some fish parents lay and fertilize millions of eggs, and let the eggs float away to hatch. Because the eggs are unprotected from hungry **predators**, only a

Feathers and Fur

Birds and mammals have backbones and can control their body temperature without needing to sit in the sun or hide in the shade. Most birds bring food to their chicks. Mammals have fur, and **nurse** their young with milk.

handful of the millions of eggs laid will live to adulthood.

Once butterflies produce their eggs, the adults flutter off. After a caterpillar hatches from the egg, it's on its own. It must find its own food and stay away from danger. Most of the caterpillars don't live long enough to become adult butterflies.

All **mammals** and most birds do things differently. Parents care for the babies until they are able to survive on their own. Baby-sitting is done either by both parents or by only one, usually the mother. Because each baby requires more care, mammals and birds produce fewer young.

These animal parents often make special preparations for a baby's arrival by building a nest or den. They will watch over their young for months or even years. During that time, the parents teach their youngsters survival lessons, such as how to find food, how to escape enemies, and how to fly. If the parents teach the lessons well, their offspring will survive to have their own babies.

Bring on the Baby Sitters

Animal parents that care for their young usually do all the work themselves. Some parents, however, have helpers. These helpers may feed the baby, protect it from danger, keep it warm, or even do the housekeeping.

Baby-sitting occurs in animals that live in social groups. In these groups, helpers take care of young that are not their own

Helpers for Life

In the case of social insects, such as honeybees, one female (the queen) spends most of her life laying eggs. Honeybee colony members are all sisters. They care for the eggs and their younger brothers and sisters, protect the nest, and search for food. The colony may contain twenty to forty thousand female helpers that stay as workers for their lives. They will never have young of their own.

African elephants are one of the many types of mammals that help each other raise their young.

offspring. Helpers may be the baby's older siblings, aunts and uncles, or even non-relatives.

Scientists once thought that only social insects, such as ants, termites, and some bees and wasps, used baby sitters. As they studied how other animals live, however, they realized that some birds and mammals use helpers, too.

Some bird and mammal helpers only stay around home long enough to help the parents with the next batch of babies. Others will help to raise several sets of brothers and sisters before starting their own families. In a few cases, the helpers keep the job for a lifetime and never have their own offspring.

The baby sitter sometimes pays a price for helping. For example, the baby sitter that stands guard over a nest or den often puts itself in danger. By spending time caring for the babies, a helper may have less time to get food for itself. A mother that nurses her sister's young may have less milk for her own offspring.

So why do helpers baby-sit someone else's young? How does their helping benefit the group—and themselves? By studying different kinds of animals in their natural homes, scientists have found some answers to these questions.

Baby Sitters Wanted

Baby sitters are more common in birds than in mammals. At least 250 of the 10,000 bird **species** and 65 of the 4,000 mammal species have baby sitters.

Females in a lion pride raise their cubs with help from their mother, aunts, and sisters.

Chapter Two

Moms Helping Moms

Mothers sometimes care for each other's young. These mothers are usually related. They may be sisters. They may be a mother and daughters, or aunts and nieces. By baby-sitting for their relatives, these animals improve the chances that their family's babies will survive. Many very different species of animals use this strategy—from the powerful African lion to the small prairie dog to the huge sperm whale!

The African Lion

Lions live in the open woodlands and grasslands of central and southern Africa in groups called **prides**. Prides may range in size from three or four individuals to several dozen. The female lions and their cubs make up the majority of the pride. A female stays in her pride for her entire life, which can be about 15 years in the wild.

The African lions hunt zebra, antelope, buffalo, and warthogs. Females do most of the hunting for the pride.

The males in a pride are not related to the females. They are related to each other, though, usually as brothers. In most prides, one male is **dominant** to the other males. As the most powerful male, he influences their behavior.

Lionesses begin to mate at age 3 or 4. All female lions in a pride have their cubs at about the same time of year. After a 3- to 4-month **pregnancy**, each lioness brings her two to three

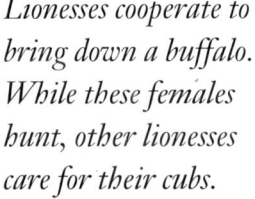

Lionesses cooperate to bring down a buffalo. While these females hunt, other lionesses care for their cubs.

newborn cubs to the pride nursery. By keeping the cubs in one place, the mother lions can more easily protect them from predators such as hyenas or from male lions from outside the pride that may try to kill them. While some of the mothers hunt together, other lionesses nurse and protect all the cubs. If a cub survives to 2 years of age—and only 20 percent of lion cubs survive that long—it will be able to hunt and take care of itself.

Adult males kick the young males out of the pride before they reach 3 years old. Later, working in groups of two to six, these young males—often brothers—try to take over other prides from older males. If they win, they kill all the nursing cubs and mate with the lionesses.

When lionesses baby-sit for each other, all the young in the pride have a better chance of survival. The cubs receive more nourishment, and are protected from predators and invading

An Unusual Situation

Most mammal mothers won't nurse another mother's young, but lionesses will nurse cubs of close relatives.

Male lions fight for control of the pride. The winner mates with the lionesses.

male lions. In the dangerous **habitat** where lions live, it pays to have help.

The African Elephant

It takes a whole herd to raise a baby elephant. The herd is made up of related females, called cows, and their young, called calves. It includes sisters, mothers and daughters, and the offspring of all these female elephants. By helping to raise one another's babies, the cows improve the chances that each calf will survive.

A mother elephant's pregnancy lasts for nearly 2 years, and an elephant cow gives birth to just one calf every 4 or 5 years. The newborn calf weighs more than 200 pounds (91 kilograms). It will drink milk from its mother for a long time, 2 to 3 years. It nurses by using its mouth, not its trunk. An elephant's trunk is actually its upper lip and nose. After 3 or 4 months of life, the calf begins to eat plant material.

All the cows work together to raise the herd's young. They get help from the young elephants who have not yet begun to **breed**, or have their own babies. The helpers baby-sit their brothers and sisters, nieces and nephews, and cousins. Young females help more than young males.

Big Eaters

Elephants are the largest of the land mammals. They **forage** for food for up to 16 hours a day, eating grasses, leaves, and woody parts of trees and shrubs. Elephants damaged the tree shown here during foraging.

The elephant family protects calves from predators, such as lions, hyenas, and humans, by forming a defensive circle around the young. If one member of the herd is injured, others in the group often come to her aid. If a calf gets stuck in the mud, baby sitters will pull it out.

Growing Up

Male elephants, or bulls, spend most of their time living alone, joining female groups only to mate. They chase away rival males. Once the young males in the herd reach maturity, at around 14 years of age, they will be chased away too. These young males will try to find mates in a different herd.

Females begin to breed after age 10. If a female survives until age 50, she stops having babies, but continues to help her sisters, daughters, and granddaughters raise their young. As the oldest member of the group, she knows where the best food and water can be found and how to avoid danger.

Despite their complex social system for protecting young, elephants are threatened. Although they can live 60 years in the wild, half of them die before age 15. Many are killed for their ivory tusks. Others starve when their habitats are destroyed, since elephants need large areas for grazing.

An elephant mother feeds her calf. The baby uses its mouth to nurse, not its trunk.

Baby-Sitting Beneath the Sea

Some large sea mammals have a social life like that of the elephant. Killer whales live in family groups of ten to thirty members. They work together to care for the young. When a mother whale dives for food, another whale stays on the surface with her baby, protecting it from predators. Pilot and sperm whales also use baby sitters.

The Black-Tailed Prairie Dog

Like female lions and elephants, prairie dog females cooperate to raise their young. Prairie dog mothers aren't always quite as helpful to their kin, though. In fact, they will sometimes kill a relative's babies.

Prairie dogs, which are **rodents**, live in "towns" on the Great Plains from Canada to Mexico. The short prairie grasses and seeds provide their food. Each town is made of several hundred individuals living in **coteries**, or family groups.

Each coterie contains one dominant male, who has won his position by fighting. The rest of the coterie includes three or

four adult females and their young. The females are relatives —mothers, daughters, sisters. The members of the coterie groom each other and identify family members by a "kiss." Together, they chase intruders away.

A coterie has its own **territory**, which includes a series of separate tunnels. Each tunnel is about 15 to 30 feet (5 to 10 meters) long with two or three entrances, and extends 6 to 9 feet (2 to 3 m) underground. The coterie's territory is passed from generation to generation.

Prairie dogs only leave their tunnels during the day, when they can spot danger. A **sentinel** prairie dog keeps watch for enemies by sitting on a mound of dirt piled at the tunnel entrance. The added height lets the sentinel see above the grass. Predators include **raptors** (hawks, eagles, falcons), bobcats, badgers, rattlesnakes, and coyotes.

An adult black-tailed prairie dog and several pups sit on a mound of dirt by the entrance to their tunnel.

An alert black-tailed prairie dog keeps a cautious eye on a gopher snake. The prairie dog's shrill whistle alerts others that danger is near.

When the sentinel spots danger, it gives an alarm call that reports the predator's size and speed. The shrill whistles set off a chain reaction of warning calls throughout the town. The other prairie dogs, alerted by the alarm, have time to run for cover in the tunnels. Since a prairie dog's only effective defense against predators is hiding, this group warning system increases the chances that the prairie dog's family will survive.

Plowmen of the Plains

Prairie dogs are sometimes called the "Plowmen of the Plains" because they keep the soil mixed and fertile by their digging.

The Birth Season

Prairie dogs mate underground in late winter. Each female has her own nest tunnel. After about a month, she gives birth to a **litter** of four or five pups in a grass-lined nesting chamber deep in her tunnel. The pups won't go above ground until they are 6 weeks old.

While the pups are still underground, mother prairie dogs sometimes sneak into neighboring tunnels of their coterie where they kill and eat the babies of their relatives. Two-thirds of the young may be killed.

No one is sure why a female would kill and eat her own nieces, nephews, brothers, or sisters. This strange behavior may be related to food shortages. Despite this behavior, when the pups emerge from the tunnels a few weeks later, the danger from relatives is past. Each female will care for and protect any of the surviving pups in the coterie. Like lions, prairie dog females will even nurse their relatives' babies.

Young males leave the coterie after 12 to 14 months, kicked out by the dominant male. They will try to take over another coterie from an older male. Female prairie dogs begin to breed at age 2 years. They will spend their entire lives in the coterie where they were born, often helping to raise their relatives' young.

A Shrinking Habitat

Two hundred years ago, there may have been five billion prairie dogs in the United States. Their towns reached for over 100 miles (160 kilometers). Today, prairie dog habitat has been reduced by the spread of farms and suburbs, and the animal's survival is threatened. When prairie dog numbers dwindled, their major predator—the black-footed ferret—nearly became extinct.

A Florida scrub jay carries an acorn in its beak. Florida scrub jay parents get most of their baby-sitting help from their older sons.

Chapter Three

Family Ties in the Air

When female mammals work together to raise young, the males often keep their distance. In bird societies, however, males are more likely to baby-sit than females are. If bird parents have helpers, they might be the older sons of the breeding pair, or they could be part of a large family group including uncles, brothers, and sometimes sisters or aunts. Acorn woodpeckers, Florida scrub jays, and American crows are all species of birds that use baby sitters.

The Acorn Woodpecker

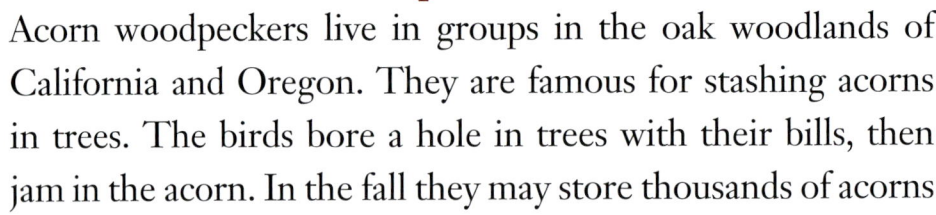

A California acorn woodpecker perches on a tree containing its family's winter acorn supply.

Acorn woodpeckers live in groups in the oak woodlands of California and Oregon. They are famous for stashing acorns in trees. The birds bore a hole in trees with their bills, then jam in the acorn. In the fall they may store thousands of acorns in a single storage tree. This enables them to stay in the same area throughout the winter and spring when food is hard to find.

A woodpecker group contains the **breeders**, who produce the young, and up to ten non-breeding helpers. The helpers usually are the young from previous years. One to four related males breed with the females. The male breeders usually are brothers, but sometimes are a father and sons. The one to three female breeders usually are sisters. The male and female breeders are not related to each other.

Each spring the breeding males compete to mate with the females. Then all breeders in the flock make a single nest in a tree hole. After the nest is built, the females begin to lay eggs in it.

In about one-quarter of acorn woodpecker groups, more than one female in the group lays eggs in the same nest. When that happens, the egg toss begins. Using their beaks, the females remove eggs from the nest, destroying a third of the eggs laid. A female continues tossing eggs until she starts to lay her own eggs in the nest. This killing of a relative's young is similar to the behavior of the prairie dog.

At the end of the egg-laying period, the three to six eggs left in the nest often are from different parents. Despite the earlier egg tossing, all the breeders now take turns sitting on the eggs, whether the eggs are theirs or not. Two weeks later, the eggs hatch. The breeders and non-breeding helpers bring food to the babies, called **nestlings**, keep them warm, and protect them from predators.

Non-breeders have to wait for their turn to breed. If there is no territory with plentiful food nearby, they stay with their family group where they will be more likely to survive. If the opposite sex parent dies and is replaced by a bird from outside the family group, a helper may breed with the newcomer. Otherwise, the non-breeder waits until a breeder dies in a nearby territory, and then moves there. By age 3, female helpers have either become breeders at home or have left the flock. By age 4, the male helpers have left, too.

Despite the competition to mate and lay eggs, acorn woodpeckers work together to store acorns, defend their territory, and raise young. Helpers—the more the better—help to ensure that the group's young survive, especially in years when food is scarce.

Different Home, Different Social Life

Not all acorn woodpeckers have helpers. Those living in the milder **climates** of the southwestern United States, Mexico, and Central America do not. Because the weather is warmer, food is available year round. Scientists guess that these woodpeckers don't need helpers because they don't have to collect and guard a stash of acorns for cold weather times.

The Florida Scrub Jay

The Florida scrub jays nest in oak scrub and short palmetto trees on ancient sand dunes in Florida. They eat acorns, insects, lizards, and snakes.

The jays live in family groups headed by a breeding pair that stays together from year to year. Non-breeding helpers, usually the young from previous years, make up the rest of the group. About half of breeding pairs have at least one helper, and sometimes they have as many as eight.

The jay family stays in its territory year round. All members of the group defend the territory against other jays by

Scientists attached a yellow identification band to this Florida scrub jay's leg in order to find out where the bird travels.

squawking and attacking intruders with their bills, claws, and wings. Group members also take turns as sentinels, watching for predators. Hawks are the major threat—they eat both adults and nestlings.

In March, the breeding pair of jays builds a new nest of twigs in a scrubby tree. The female breeder lays an average of three to four eggs and **incubates** them for 18 days. After the eggs hatch, her mate brings food to her and the nestlings while she continues to sit on the nest. After another 18 days, the young are able to fly.

During the breeding period, the helpers stand guard, attack invaders, and bring food to the nestlings. They do not build or sit on the nest, though. Their main job is giving warnings and keeping away predators. Breeders who have helpers produce more young. This is because fewer eggs and nestlings are lost to predators.

> **Helpers at the Nest**
>
> Other birds that have baby sitters are the Mexican jay, kookaburra, Galapagos mockingbird, African wood hoopoe, pied kingfisher, Harris' hawk, and white-fronted bee-eater.

Leaving Home

Female helpers usually leave the family after a year, and try to find another group that has lost its female breeder. If they fail to join a new group, they die. The male helpers, however, stay closer to home and wait until a breeding territory opens up nearby. This may happen after a couple years—or it may never happen.

Empty territories are hard to find because the jays are restricted to small, scattered patches of scrub. Other jay families already occupy most good territory in the area. Since a

Florida scrub jay can live up to 15 years, territories don't often change owners.

Scrub jays do not mate with their relatives. So if either the male or female breeder dies, a new mate comes in from outside the family's territory. A male helper's only chance to take over his family territory comes if both parents die. The oldest son usually inherits the territory, then accepts a mate from another territory.

A male helper has a chance to move away if the male breeder in a neighboring territory is sick or dies. Then his parents will fight neighbors to help their son get breeding space. Over his lifetime, he has a better chance of surviving and breeding if he stays home and helps his parents to raise their young.

A crow nestling begs for food. In some crow families, baby sitters help feed the young and protect them from predators, such as raccoons, squirrels, and raptors.

The American Crow

Crows live throughout North America. Those found in Canada migrate south before the severe winter chill sets in. In areas with milder temperatures, though, crows stay in one area year round.

As among the acorn woodpeckers, the lifestyle of crows varies depending on where they live. In some areas, the breeding pair mates for life and raises its chicks alone. In other places, baby sitters help their parents to raise the young. No one is sure why these differences exist, although they probably involve conditions such as food and territory availability.

Each spring the breeding pair builds a nest of sticks and twigs high in a tree. The female crow lays two to six eggs and incubates them for about 19 days. Her mate feeds her while she sits on the nest. After hatching, the young need care until they are 6 to 8 weeks old. During this time, the parents do most of the work.

Families with Helpers

When helpers are part of the family group, there are usually one or two baby sitters. Crow families, though, can have as many as thirteen helpers. Baby sitters are usually the young from previous years. They help feed nestlings, defend the territory, and protect the young from predators.

Like acorn woodpeckers and Florida scrub jays, crows do not mate with relatives. Helpers find mates in other family groups. Females usually move out after 2 or 3 years, find a territory where a female breeder has died, and begin breeding. As in scrub jays, they usually move farther from home than their brothers do.

The male helpers often stay with their family for 4 to 6 years, and on average don't breed until they're nearly 5 years old. A male helper is likely to find a new territory close to his parents' home. He may also inherit his parents' territory. This may be the major advantage to staying home.

African wild dog parents get pup care from baby sitters. These pups excitedly greet two adults.

Chapter Four

Staying Home with Mom and Dad

Most mammal mothers have a different mate each breeding season and raise their babies alone. Once the male and female mate, the male leaves the female to raise the young by herself. In some mammal species, though, the breeding pair stays together for more than one season, and gets baby-sitting help from close family members. Cotton-top tamarins, pygmy marmosets, and African wild dogs all get extra help in raising their young.

The Cotton-Top Tamarin

Among **primates,** such as apes and monkeys, it is unusual to find males, either fathers or young non-breeders, helping to raise babies. Males are key helpers in some species of tamarins and marmosets, though.

The cotton-top tamarin is found in the rain forests of Colombia. It uses its long tail to keep its balance as it jumps and climbs in the treetops. Cotton-tops eat insects and fruit.

The cotton-top lives in family groups of one breeding female, her mate, and their offspring from the previous years. The average group size is six animals, not including newborns.

The young cotton-top tamarin rides on the back of a baby sitter until it is old enough to jump and climb in the treetops on its own.

The mother gives birth after about 5 months of pregnancy, usually to twins. Because the group travels to avoid predators and to find food, the babies must be carried through the treetops all the time. The youngsters cling to the backs of their older siblings or their father.

Besides carrying the infant cotton-tops, baby sitters groom them, keep them warm, and play with them. They return the babies to the mother for nursing. Once the babies can eat solid food, the baby sitters will share food with them. Helpers also watch out for the tamarin's predators—snakes and raptors. After 3 months, the babies can get around well on their own.

A tamarin mother could not raise her young without help. The father's efforts help to ensure that his babies survive. Extra assistance from older siblings eases the load on both parents, too.

Cotton-top tamarin groups with more helpers have better success in raising young. In one study, 70 percent of infants survived when there were three or four helpers. Just 40 percent of the babies lived when only the two parents cared for them.

Daughters are able to breed by the age of 18 months. As long as they live in the family group, though, they do not breed. The mother prevents her daughters from producing young by a scent signal, backed up by physical aggression if necessary. Sons do not try to breed while living at home, either.

Watch Out!

Tamarins have different alarm calls for predators in the air and those on the ground. The different calls tell their family which direction—up or down—to move to safety.

Most daughters and sons stay home until they are 3 or 4 years old. Then they will leave the family in search of a mate and a territory. The experience they gain from baby-sitting their brothers and sisters seems to help them be more successful as parents.

The Pygmy Marmoset

The pygmy marmoset is the world's smallest primate. It lives high in the canopy of tropical rain forests in South America. Like the tamarin, the family group contains one breeding pair plus their helpers, who are recent offspring. An average group has three or four helpers, plus one or two infants.

A baby pygmy marmoset must be carried as its family travels around the canopy of a South American rain forest.

Usually a marmoset mother has twins, and they must be carried everywhere. The mother also needs help with protection and foraging for tree sap and gum, the main foods of the pygmy marmosets. The father and the brothers and sisters take over all the childcare duties except nursing. The young ride on the baby sitters' backs until they are almost 2 months old.

The helpers will stay at home until they find their own breeding territory, usually when they are around 2 years of age. By helping with childcare, they rear more little brothers and sisters—and learn to be better parents.

What's for Dinner?
Working together, African wild dogs hunt zebras, gazelles, and young wildebeests.

The African Wild Dog

African wild dogs live in groups called **packs** that stay together year round. An average pack contains two breeders and five or six helpers. Most helpers are males, although a few may be young females born in the previous year. The wild dogs hunt together, enabling them to catch prey that a single wild dog couldn't bring down alone.

A pack of wild dogs usually has only one breeding female. Her mate, the dominant male, is not related to her. The male helpers include their sons and her mate's brothers. The dominant male prevents his brothers from mating with the breeding female by using threatening stares or force. The female's sons do not try to mate with her, either.

After a pregnancy of about 10 weeks, the female wild dog gives birth to a litter of nine to twelve pups. Usually only one litter is born each season. While the mother nurses the pups in the den, the father and helpers bring her food.

An African wild dog grooms a pup. Baby sitters also help to feed and protect the pups.

At the age of 3 or 4 weeks, the nursing pups begin eating meat, too. The pack members take turns bringing food to the pups. They carry meat from the hunting grounds in their stomachs, then spit up the meat for the puppies. Helpers also groom the pups and play with them. They chase away predators, such as hyenas, jackals, lions, and cheetahs. When the pack goes off to hunt, one or two helpers stay behind to baby-sit.

African wild dogs reach maturity at about 2 years of age. Young females leave the group, searching for a pack without a breeder. Sometimes a female tries to join a pack that already has a breeder. If she succeeds in joining, the dominant female in that pack usually stops her from breeding.

Some males may also leave the family to join new packs, although they usually remain close by. Most males stay in the home pack to help.

The pack is more successful in raising pups if it has adult helpers. Extra helpers are able to bring more food back to the pups, protect them from predators, and teach them how to hunt successfully.

Cousins with the Same Family Life

The wolf, red fox, coyote, and the silver-backed and golden jackal also have baby sitters, most of which are males.

A family group of meerkats watches for danger in southern Africa. Like their relatives the dwarf mongooses, meerkats live in large colonies and use baby sitters to raise the young.

Chapter Five

Safety in Numbers

Sometimes, just a few helpers aren't enough. Larger groups can devote more individuals to gathering food or protecting the young than smaller groups can. That may mean that the entire group, and all the offspring, has a better chance of survival. A family group of mammals can be as large as a pack of a dozen members or a colony of several dozen. The breeding pair in these groups depends on many baby sitters to help raise the young.

The Dwarf Mongoose

The dwarf mongoose is found in open woodland of sub-Saharan Africa. It nests in the airshafts of termite mounds. The animals stay in the mounds during the night, coming out to search for food during the day.

Dwarf mongooses scramble up the outside of their termite mound home.

Dwarf mongooses live in packs with one breeding pair. Most groups also contain six or seven non-breeding helpers, usually the offspring of the breeding pair. Occasionally, unrelated helpers may join the pack.

The breeding female gives birth to two or three litters, each having an average of three babies, during the October-May rainy season. Each pregnancy lasts 7 weeks. The newborn dwarf mongooses are blind and hairless. They can't forage with the pack until they are 6 weeks old. The young spend their days in the termite mound airshafts.

That's where the baby sitters come in handy. While the parents forage for food, the male and female helpers take turns caring for the young. The helpers carry, groom, guard, and feed insects to the babies. Since the help means a mother is able to eat more food, she can provide more milk for her babies and produce more litters.

The breeding male physically stops the other males in the pack from mating. He also chases outsider males away. The dominant, breeding female usually doesn't allow helper females to produce

A Bug Lover

The dwarf mongoose's sharp, pointed teeth are perfect for eating small insects, termites, grasshoppers, and beetles.

Friend of the Family

An unrelated helper gives as much care as family members do. By helping, it may become the pack's breeder.

Coping with Predators

Some species of mongooses, like this one staring down a cobra in India, live alone. Dwarf mongooses, however, are found in Africa and live in family groups that work together to survive.

Dwarf mongooses hunt during the day and can be easily spotted by predators. Living in a group provides these small animals with extra protection through alarm calls and group attacks.

young. If one does mate and produce a litter, the dominant female often kills the young. If food is plentiful, however, she may let the helper breed in order to keep her in the pack. Good help is hard to find.

Most dwarf mongoose helpers eventually leave home between 2 and 3 years of age. Some, especially males, meet a helper of the opposite sex from a different pack. Together they start a new pack in an unoccupied territory. Other helpers join existing packs and wait for their chance to breed.

Baby sitters that stay at home get a chance to breed if both parents die. A daughter—usually the oldest—may then succeed her mother, or the oldest son will succeed his father as the dominant male. They will mate with an unrelated mongoose that has been helping the pack.

Group living protects dwarf mongooses from predators, such as raptors, jackals, cheetahs, and the snakes that crawl into their dens. Larger packs are more successful in protecting their young, in alerting each other to danger with alarm calls, and in attacking invading snakes. Therefore, they raise more young than unaided pairs.

The Naked Mole-Rat

The naked mole-rat lives in dry areas of northeastern Africa. These rodents build an elaborate tunnel system that can stretch as far as 2 miles (3 km). The mole-rats expand their tunnels in search of roots and tubers, their source of food and water. They survive by living in large groups and working together to search for food and fight off predators.

Naked mole-rat colonies usually have seventy-five to eighty members. Some colonies have as many as three hundred. One female, the queen, gives birth to all the young.

The other members of the colony are helpers. They care for the pups, gather food, dig tunnels, and protect the colony

Naked mole-rats from two different colonies face off before fighting. Naked mole-rats recognize colony mates by smell and attack strangers.

from snakes. Each has a specific job, which can change over its lifetime. The queen makes sure the helpers do their jobs by shoving and nipping them.

The colony has one to three breeding males who were once helpers. After the queen chooses them as mates, their only job is to breed with her and care for the pups. These males are usually closely related to the queen, and may even be her brothers.

The queen has four to five litters a year, each containing ten to fifteen pups. She nurses the pups herself. The male

Naked mole-rats huddle together in their colony's nest chamber.

breeders and workers help her groom and protect them. After 1 month the pups stop nursing and eat solid food. By 2 months, they begin working as helpers in the colony.

All the helpers are physically able to breed, but most never will. The queen stops other females from mating and from threatening her throne by pushing and shoving them. The males rarely fight with each other for the right to breed.

If the queen becomes weak or dies, a battle for power begins. The largest females, who often are sisters, fight each other by shoving, biting, or fencing with their teeth. Finally,

Mighty Teeth

Naked mole-rats dig tunnels in the brick-hard soil with their razor-sharp teeth.

A Hairier Mole-Rat

Damaraland mole-rats, from the Kalahari Desert of southern Africa, also live in underground colonies. Unlike naked mole-rats, they are covered with fur. Colonies consist of a breeding pair and ten to fourteen helpers. Helpers do the housekeeping, digging, and baby-sitting.

Damaraland mole-rats will not mate with their parents or siblings the way naked mole-rats will. If a parent dies, the helpers leave the colony. During the rainy season, a single Damaraland mole-rat is able to dig a tunnel. It tries to find a mate or moves to a colony without a breeder.

one female wins by injuring, killing, or frightening the others. She will become the next mother of the colony.

Why Stick Around?

Naked mole-rats live in hot, dry climates where food is widely spread out, the soil is hard to dig, and dangerous snakes are present. Helpers rarely leave the safety of their colony. The ground is too hard for one animal to dig a tunnel alone. Besides, neighboring naked mole-rats will kill a visitor that is not part of their colony. A single naked mole-rat has a slim chance of surviving long enough to dig a new tunnel, locate food, find a mate, and raise its young.

Sticking around the colony can pay off for the naked mole-rat helper. It may eventually get a chance to produce its own young if one of the breeders dies. Waiting for this opportunity and helping its queen mother rear little brothers and sisters is its safest bet.

A wolf pack hunts in snowy Montana. Wolves rely on baby sitters to help raise the young.

Chapter Six

Why Do They Help?

Scientists have observed helping behavior in a wide range of species. Animals that have baby sitters may be tiny honeybees or huge elephants. These animals may eat acorns or insects or freshly killed meat. Animals that have baby sitters live in widely different habitats, from the deserts of Africa to the rain forests of South America to woodlands of California. So what do all these cooperative animals have in common?

One Kind of Animal, Many Lifestyles

Thirty-five of the 1,700 species of rodents use baby sitters. Social groups can be quite different, though. For example, closely related house mouse females raise their young in the same nest and nurse each other's babies. The naked mole-rat colony includes only one breeding female and dozens of helpers that will never breed themselves.

It's All About the Neighborhood

Living in a group helps all these social animals survive. Because of conditions in the environment, a single animal would have less success finding food, avoiding predators, and raising its young on its own.

For example, food might be so spread out that one individual would die before it found any. If a group searches, though, as the naked mole-rats do, there is more chance that one will find enough for the group to share. For hunting animals, such as the African wild dogs and African lions, the **prey** may be too large to catch without help.

Avoiding danger may require a similar group effort. A single animal can be too small to fight off a predator alone, but several animals together can chase away or kill the enemy. That's how the naked mole-rats and dwarf mongooses do it. In a group, a guard can watch for danger while the others eat—a strategy used by the prairie dog, scrub jay, and pygmy marmoset.

In some cases, the family group sticks together because there's nowhere for the kids to move. Florida scrub jays, for example, live in an area in which most territories are already occupied by other jays. The young stay home where they already have food and protection. Then when a neighboring territory opens up, their family will help them take it over.

The environment of the neighborhood determines how large the social group is, how long the helpers stay at home, and how much they help with the young.

Elephant baby sitters form a protective circle around a calf to shield it from predators.

What's in It for the Baby Sitter?

The baby sitter's best chance of survival might be to stay in its family group, even if that means having to help out with new babies. Leaving home may be dangerous because locating food, avoiding predators, and finding a mate is risky. Neighboring groups may not welcome the newcomer, and may even try to kill it. Good living territories may be hard to find.

Staying home for a while gives the baby sitter a safe place to mature and grow stronger. Then, when it's ready to leave home in search of a mate and new territory, it may be more successful. In some cases, baby sitters get a chance to inherit the family territory and to breed there. This is easier than fighting to gain a territory elsewhere.

A helper may get other benefits from helping to raise its relatives, especially its brothers and sisters. By developing skills, such as finding food, defending the group, and giving care, the baby sitter may do a better job of raising its own young. These skills may even help the baby sitter impress a potential mate. Later, those younger brothers and sisters may end up helping the baby sitter raise its own young, as they wait for their turn to breed.

Sometimes, taking care of a relative's baby means that the relative returns the favor. Then both parents' offspring have a better chance of surviving. The African lion, elephant, and prairie dog all work this way. Even when a baby sitter has little chance of breeding itself, as among the naked mole-rats, helping to raise close relatives is another way to continue its family's line to the next generation.

What's in It for the Family?

Having the extra helpers benefits the family, too. A pair of cotton-top tamarins or pygmy marmosets would have trouble finding food, avoiding predators, and caring for their twins without help. The more helpers they have, the more likely

---

Helping the Disappearing Species

Many of the animals discussed in this book are threatened or endangered, including the cotton-top tamarin, Florida scrub jay, African elephant, African wild dog, and black-tailed prairie dog. When habitat is destroyed by human activity, these animals cannot find enough food. Without adequate breeding territories, they cannot raise families. By understanding how they live and by protecting habitats from destruction, we may be able to help these animals survive.

their babies will survive. The African lion or dwarf mongoose mother has more time to find food for herself if a helper watches her babies. This enables her to produce more milk and raise healthier babies.

Acorn woodpecker parents need helpers to collect and protect their stash of acorns, or they and their offspring could starve. A prairie dog family has a better chance of escaping swooping predators if there are "watch dogs" on alert. An African wild dog needs support from others in order to hunt. For these social animals, living in a family of helpers benefits everyone.

More to Learn

Studying animals in the wild is difficult. It takes many hours of careful observation to understand an animal's social life. The scientist's job is even harder if the animal lives under the ocean like the whale, underground like the naked mole-rat, in the thick jungle like the cotton-top tamarin, or in a large territory like the American crow.

As the social lives of more birds and mammals are studied, other animal baby sitters will surely be discovered. You might even be the scientist who makes the discovery!

An adult coyote and pup greet each other. Like African dogs and wolves, coyotes rely on baby sitters to help raise the young.

Glossary

breed—to produce young

breeder—an animal that produces young

climate—weather conditions, such as temperature, rainfall, humidity

coterie—a family group of prairie dogs

dominant—the individual in a group that has the most power or influence over the others

forage—to search for food

habitat—the area in which an animal normally lives

incubate—to sit on and hatch eggs

litter—a group of young mammals born at the same time from the same mother

mammal—an animal that has hair on its body, gives birth to live young, and feeds its young with mother's milk

nestling—a young bird not yet ready to leave the nest

nurse—to feed milk to the young

pack—a group of animals that live and hunt together

predator—an animal that hunts other animals for food

pregnancy—the length of time required for a mammal to develop inside its mother's body before birth

prey—an animal hunted by other animals

pride—a group of lions

primate—a group of mammals that has flexible hands and feet; includes humans, apes, and monkeys

raptor—a bird of prey including hawks, eagles, falcons

rodents—the scientific order of gnawing mammals

sentinel—a guard that watches for danger, especially predators

species—a group of animals that can mate and produce fertile young

territory—the area in which an animal finds food, breeds, and sleeps

To Find Out More

Books and Periodicals

Birds: Their Life, Their Ways, Their World. Pleasantville, NY: The Reader's Digest Association, Inc., 1979.

Dodd, Catherine. "Making Room for Prairie Dogs." *Smithsonian*, March 1998: 60–68.

Jarrow, Gail and Paul Sherman. *The Naked Mole-Rat Mystery, Scientific Sleuths at Work.* Minneapolis: Lerner Publications Company, 1996.

Joubert, Dereck. *Hunting with the Moon: The Lions of Savuti.* Washington: National Geographic Society, 1997.

MacDonald, David, editor. *The Encyclopedia of Mammals*, second edition. New York: Facts on File, 2001.

McNutt, John and Lesley Boggs. *Running Wild: Dispelling the Myths of the African Wild Dog.* Washington: Smithsonian Institution, 1996.

Patent, Dorothy Hinshaw. *Prairie Dogs.* Boston: Houghton Mifflin, 1999.

Organizations and Online Sites

The Audubon Society
http://www.audubon.org
This organization is an excellent source of information about birds and bird watching.

Crows
http://cumv.bio.cornell.edu/mcgowan/crowinfo.htm
This site by Dr. Kevin McGowan, of the Cornell University Museum of Vertebrates, discusses American crows and their behavior.

Encyclopedia Britannica
http://www.britannica.com
This informational site provides links to the *Encyclopedia Britannica* and to related web sites about animals.

Florida Fish and Wildlife Conservation Commission
http://fcn.state.fl.us/gfc/viewing/species/jay.html
This site contains photographs and information about the Florida scrub jay.

Lincoln Park Zoo, Chicago
http://www.lpzoo.com
This site features photographs and details about many species of animals. Learn about an animal's social life, habitat, food source, and predators.

Smithsonian Institution and National Zoo
http://www.si.edu/natzoo/
The National Zoo site contains information, photographs, and web links about animals covered in this book. Watch live Webcams of naked mole-rats, elephants, and other animals in the zoo.

U.S. Fish and Wildlife Service
http://www.fws.gov
This United States government agency has information on endangered species, habitat conservation, and more.

A Note on Sources

To research this book, we went to the best, most accurate sources we could find—the scientists who study the animals. Because much of the information about animal baby sitters is brand new, we didn't rely on encyclopedias or general reference books. Instead, we read books and articles written by scientists who had spent years studying the animals' behavior. Since Paul is a scientist himself, he knows what research has been done, and personally knows many of the scientists who study animal behavior.

For an overview of the subject, we used two books that discussed some of the research about animal helpers: *Cooperative Breeding in Mammals*, edited by Nancy G. Solomon and Jeffrey A. French, and *Cooperative Breeding in Birds*, edited by Peter B. Stacey and Walter D. Koenig. In the Cornell University library we tracked down detailed articles by scientists who were experts on the animals in our book.

We also relied on firsthand research. Paul has studied naked mole-rats for over 20 years, and has six colonies of the rodents in his laboratory at Cornell University. To learn about the crow, we talked to Dr. Kevin McGowan, who has spent 10 years investigating the bird's social system. Dr. John Hoogland provided facts about prairie dogs based on his observations of the animals in South Dakota. Drs. Frank Pitelka and Walter Koenig supplied information on acorn woodpeckers, based on 25 years of research. Gail went to the American Ornithological Union meeting and listened to Dr. Glen Woolfenden summarize his 30 years of research on the Florida scrub jay.

As result of our research, everything you read in this book is the most up-to-date information we could find.

—Gail Jarrow and Paul Sherman

Index

Numbers in *italics* indicate illustrations.

Acorn woodpeckers, 24–25, *24*, 53
  breeders, 24
  egg tossing, 25
  egg-laying, 24–25
  helpers, 24–25
  nestlings, 25
  nests, 24
African elephants, *10*, 16–17, *17*, *51*, 52
  breeding, 16–17
  bulls, 17
  calves, 16, *17*
  cows, 16–17, *17*
  herds, 16
  nursing, 16
  predators, 17
African lions, 14–16, *15*, 50, 52–53
  cubs, 15
  dominant males, 14
  predators, 15
  pregnancy, 14–15
  prides, 14
African wild dogs, *30*, *35*, 35–37, *36*, 50, 52–53
  breeding, 35–36
  diet, *35*, 37
  helpers, 35, 37
  packs, 35
American crows, 28–29, *28*
  helpers, 29
  nests, *28*

Birds, 8, *8*, 10–11, *22*, *23*, 26–29, 53
Black-tailed prairie dogs, 18–21, *19*, *20*, 52
  breeding, 21
  coteries, 18–19, 21
  litters, 21
  predators, 19–21

Black-tailed prairie dogs (*continued*)
  sentinels, 19–20
  territories, 19
  tunnels, 19
Butterflies, 8

Cotton-top tamarins, 32–34, *32*, 52–53
  alarm calls, 33
  diet, 32–33
  helpers, 33
  predators, 33

Damaraland mole-rats, 46
Dens, 8
Dogs. *See* African wild dogs.
Dwarf mongooses, 40–43, *40–41*, 50, 53
  diet, 41
  helpers, 41–43
  predators, 42–43, *42*
  pregnancy, 41
  teeth, 41

Egg tossing, 25
Eggs, 7–8, 25
Elephants. *See* African elephants.

Florida scrub jays, *22*, 23, 26–28, *26*, 50–52
  helpers, 26–28
  incubation period, 27
  mating period, 28
  sentinels, 27
  territories, 27–28
  territory, 26–27
foraging, 16

Helpers, 9–11, 39
  acorn woodpeckers, 24–25
  African wild dogs, 35, 37
  American crows, 29
  cotton-top tamarins, 33
  dwarf mongooses, 41–43
  Florida scrub jays, 27–28
  insects, 9
  mates, 29
  naked mole-rats, 43
Honeybees, *9*

Insects, 6, 8–10, *9*, 32

Killer whales, 18

Lions. *See* African lions.

Mammals, 8, 10–11, 18, *18*

Meerkats, *38*

Naked mole-rats, 43–47, *44, 45*, 50, 52–53
  colonies, 43
  helpers, 43, 47
  mating, 44
  nursing, 44
  queens, 44–47
  teeth, 45
Nests, 8
Nursing, 8, 15–16, 44

Pilot whales, 18
Prairie dogs, 50, 52–53

Predators, 7, 19–21, 42, *42*, 50–51, 53
Pygmy marmosets, *34*, 50, 52
  diet, 35
  helpers, 34

Rodents, 18, 43

Sea mammals, 18, *18*
Spiders, *6*

Whales, 53
Wolves, *48*. *See also* African wild dogs.

About the Authors

Gail Jarrow is the author of several novels for young readers as well as numerous magazine articles and stories. Before becoming an author, she taught science and math in elementary and middle schools. She received her undergraduate degree in zoology from Duke University and her master's degree from Dartmouth College. She and her husband have three children.

Paul Sherman is Professor of Animal Behavior at Cornell University. He earned his undergraduate degree at Stanford University, and his doctorate in zoology at the University of Michigan. Dr. Sherman is the author of over 125 scientific articles, mainly on the social behavior of birds and mammals. He and his wife have two children.

Working together, the authors have written several science articles and two award-winning books for young readers: *The Naked Mole-Rat Mystery* and *Naked Mole-Rats*. They find it easy to work together—they're next-door neighbors in rural upstate New York.